WELCOME TO THIRD EARTH! Indeed, an especially fond welcome to this, the third (and, dare we say it, greatest!) THUNDERCATS Annual. Yep – for the first time, we're proud to present an all-new package of stories featuring everyone's favourite bewhiskered super heroes – the Thundercats! All your favourites are here – there's Lion-O, Panthro, Tygra, Cheetara, Wilykat, Wilykit, Jaga and of course, Snarf. Join them in Thunder-action as we take a trip somewhere in time to the distant past of Third Earth, and the first dynasty of the dastardly devil-priest Mumm-Ra the Ever-Living! Catch up on the past history of the Cats' own planet on page 14, but don't miss our sensational text story, featuring none other than... The *Thunderdogs!* The History of Plunn-darr is covered in spine-chilling detail on page 22, and then we've a bumper 22 pages of hotter-than-hot Thundercatting, as we follow the *Fireballs of Plun-darr* across the troubled skies of Third Earth. There's a smattering of background detail to Third Earth itself on page 45 for the historians among you, and to round off those 64 sensational pages there's the concluding part of *Past Perils,* and the final fate of those Thunderdogs. That's all from us – except to remind you that you can follow the fortunes of our famed felines in Marvel's THUNDERCATS comic. For now, dim the lights, sit back, and enjoy. The action is about to begin...

THIS BOOK BELONGS TO

craig

COVER AND OPENING SPREAD ART: **STEPHEN BASKERVILLE, GEOFF SENIOR AND JOHN BURNS** EDITOR **JOHN TOMLINSON** DESIGNER **EUAN PETERS**

THUNDERCATS™ ANNUAL 1989 is published by **MARVEL COMICS LTD,** a New World company, 23 Redan Place, London W2 4SA. THUNDERCATS (including all prominent characters featured herein), and the distinctive likenesses thereof, are the trademarks of LEISURE CONCEPTS INC; TELEPICTURES CORPORATION and TED WOLF and copyright © 1988 LEISURE CONCEPTS INC; TELEPICTURES and TED WOLF. No similarity between any of the names, characters, persons and/or institutions in this book with those of any living or dead person or institution is intended, and any such similarity is purely conincidental. All rights reserved. Printed in Italy.

Script **MIKE COLLINS** ◉ Pencils **ANDY WILDMAN** ◉ Inks **MARTIN GRIFFITHS** ◉ Letters **GLOP** ◉ Colour **LOUISE CASSELL**

NIGHTFALL. A CAMP ON THE OUTSKIRTS OF A DESERT OF *PHOSPHOROUS SANDS*...

LET'S GET THIS STRAIGHT, *WYKURZ*— YOU'VE NEVER HEARD OF THE *THUNDERCATS*? BUT WE'RE KNOWN THE LENGTH AND BREADTH OF THIRD EARTH!

THAT *EXPLAINS* IT, THEN! THIS IS *FIRST* EARTH!

OH, *NO*! NOT AGAIN!

"I'VE BEEN HERE *BEFORE*, WITH THE OTHER THUNDERCATS!* WE CAME HERE TO DO BATTLE WITH THE EVIL *MUMM-RA*..."

* SEE LAST YEAR'S *THUNDERCATS* ANNUAL.

"...POSING AS THE WISE AND JUST *PHARAOH KA-REY-BAR*, HE HELD ALL OF FIRST EARTH IN A REIGN OF *TERROR*!"

TELL ME, WYKURZ— HAVE *YOU* A PHARAOH KA-REY-BAR?

INDEED *NOT*, LION-O. WE HAVE ONLY CRUEL *MUMM-RA*, WHOSE *TEMPLE* WE WERE BUILDING WHEN YOU *ARRIVED*!

BEFORE THE *ONYX PYRAMID*..? THEN OUR TASK IS *CLEAR*— TO RID FIRST *AND* THIRD EARTH OF MUMM-RA AND HIS EVIL...

...WE MUST MAKE CERTAIN THAT IT IS NEVER BUILT!

WE DO NOT *UNDERSTAND*, MIGHTY THUNDERCAT ! WHAT CAN THIS TYRANT POSSIBLY *BECOME* THAT *YOU* SPEAK OF HIM SO *FEARFULLY* ?

I CAN ONLY SHOW YOU WHAT THE PASSAGE OF *CENTURIES* WILL MAKE OF YOUR EVIL MASTER. *SWORD OF OMENS...*

...GIVE ME SIGHT *BEYOND* SIGHT !

BEHOLD — *THE EVIL OF MUMM-RA !*

AND KNOW THIS — THERE CAN BE *NO* PEACE — FOR *ANY* OF YOU — UNTIL HE IS *VANQUISHED* !

AND IN A DARK SANCTUM, NOT FAR AWAY...

BY THE CLAWS OF *KREPPLICH* ! I MUST *MODIFY* THIS ACCURSED DEVICE TO INCLUDE *SOUND* !

NO MATTER THAT I CANNOT HEAR THE *FELINE STRANGER'S* WORDS ! HE IS *TROUBLE* — AND I MUST MOBILISE MY *FORCES*...

...THE ARMIES OF *MUMM-RA, THE EVER LIVING* !

CONTINUED ON PAGE 53!

THE CHRONICLES OF THUNDERA

And it came to pass that, in the seventh quadrant of a distant galaxy, there turned a shimmering, bejewelled planet. **Thundera** was home to a great and noble race of warrior cats, but peace had reigned there for a thousand generations. The capital city of **Grimalkingrad** was a fabulous place of domes and minarets, presided over by the fabled **Cats' Lair**, seat of Imperial power on Thundera. Cats' Lair was home to the *Panthera Leo* line, noble Royal Family of Thundera, who had held the reins of power since the dawn of recorded history. Guardian of that power was **Jaga the Wise**, former **Lord of the Thundercats** and keeper of the ancient secrets of the **Eye of Thundera**. Not even Jaga knew the origin of the Eye, a great, ruby-red jewel embedded in the hilt of the mystic **Sword of Omens**. According to the **Thunderian Book Of Kings** the Eye was a gift from **Catamountain**, who lived when Thundera was young and volcanoes scarred the face of the planet. It was certainly true that Lion-O's ancestor, **Leonus the Wanderer**, had originally found the Sword of Omens in an ancient lava basin high on **Mount Grimalkin**, the dormant volcano around which Thundera's capitol was later built. Legend has it that, as Leonus chipped the Sword free of the lava, a great scarlet beam lanced into the heavens, painting the image of a cat's head across the clouds. In the roar of the thunderstorm Leonus was said to have heard the ghostly laughter of Catamountain, and when the wandering Thundercat descended from the mountain, it was as first Lord of the Thundercats. A new code was hailed the length and breadth of the land — that of **Justice, Truth, Honour and Loyalty — The Code of Thundera!**

It was many generations later that the orbit of Thundera's sun began to decay, creating immense gravitational forces which eventually tore the planet apart. Escaping the dying fires of Thundera, bringing with them the laws and ideals of their doomed planet, were **Jaga the Wise, Panthro the Deadly, Tygra the Invisible, Cheetara the Quick, Wilykat and Wilykit**, a cunning junior duo, and the **Snarf** — all sworn to serve their young Lord, **Lion-O. The Thundercats!**

Illustration: **COLLINS/BASKERVILLE** Colour: **EUAN PETERS**

THUNDERDOGS HO! PART 1

Plot **SIMON FURMAN** ● Story **MIKE COLLINS** ● Illustrations **DARREN GOODACRE** ● Colour **STEVE WHITE**

The Thundercats were enjoying a rare day of peace in the Cats' Lair, their home on Third Earth.

"I've finally got the chance to get this place fixed up," said Tygra as he and Snarf went around measuring and designing features to the Lair.

"Yes, *Snarf*, we never seem to stop! If it's not giant robots, it's earthquakes, or raiding mutants..." moaned Snarf, happy to have something to complain about.

Indeed, all the Thundercats were enjoying this surprisingly quiet period — Panthro was cleaning the Thundertank, battered and dirty from a recent battle. Lion-O and Cheetara had gone with Wilykat and Kit to gather firewood, and were now returning laden down with ample wood to last them all winter long.

"It's not often we get to just walk through Third Earth and smell the roses," mused a content Cheetara.

"Makes you wish we could just settle down here at peace, doesn't it?" said Lion-O, smiling back. They both looked into the cloudless sunny sky, watching Kat and Kit flitting by on their spaceboards.

"We missed so much, leaving Thun*dera*," sighed Cheetara.

"Well, this is our home now — we'd best make it a happy place." Lion-O tried to dispel the wistfulness in Cheetara's voice, though he felt the same longings for their long-gone home planet. "Let's hope this time lasts—"

He knew as he said it, that it was a vain hope. The peace was to be shattered all too soon...

"LION-O! Come quick!" Wilykit zipped

15

down towards them on her board, a worried expression on her face.

"What's happened?" Lion-O dropped the wood and was ready to leap into action.

"Look! There!" Cheetara and Lion-O looked toward Cats' Lair, where Wilykit was about to touch down by the prone figure of a Moleman. They raced the few dozen metres to the scene in seconds.

Inside Cats' Lair, all the Thundercats were gathered around the injured Moleman, who had been tended to by Snarf.

"Tell us what happened," inquired Panthro. The Moleman sat up on the bed they had placed him on.

"It was terrible," began the Moleman. "We suddenly found ourselves under attack from big, black bird-like things... they flew down from the sky... I ran to you... seeking help..."

There was no time to wait. Leaving Snarf to tend to the injured Moleman, the Thundercats charged off to the Molemen's pits.

"Thundercats Ho!" cried Lion-O, leading them to battle.

The Thundercats, full of energy, ready for a fight, arrived at the pits...

Only to find they weren't needed.

"What happened?" asked the confused Lion-O, the Sword of Omens held limp at his side, where seconds before it had been held high and proud. Rix, leader of the Molemen, stepped forward and talked to the Thundercats, as the black demons flew off, put to flight.

"Oh, it's you lot," he commented, offhandedly. "Well, as you can see, you're a little late to deal with our problem."

The stunned Thundercats were confused. It was a second before anyone had anything to say. Tygra spoke first...

"Who — how — what..? The demons have been driven off?"

"Yes, and without your help," said a voice from out of the pits. The Thundercats turned as one towards the source of the voice. Coming out of the pit were six figures, all dressed in exotic and dramatic armour, bejewelled and stylish. The Thundercats gaped as Rix smiled towards the approaching figures.

"May I introduce Brutus, Snarl, Cur, Imperious Rex, Mass and Wolf — the THUNDERDOGS!"

Brutus was tall, muscular, a gleaming, ruby-studded gold belt around his waist,

bright green knee-high boots. His jerkin was edged at the shoulders with yellow studs.

Snarl stooped, a strange glow in his eyes. Across his chest were several straps, each carrying a throwing weapon, a short knife in a thigh strap, and a bow slung over one shoulder. His pirate boots, jacket and trunks were leather.

Cur was swathed in a cloak, light brown in colour, underneath which various weapons were visible. He walked barefoot.

Imperious Rex was every inch the leader. Around his neck were three jewelled discs, hung on a gold chain; a vast gleaming waistband, similarly jewelled, shone so bright as to hurt the eyes. He carried, across his back, a long sword with a glittering handle. His shoulders were swathed in a short ermine cloak and, around one forearm, a gold band gleamed. He had an arrogant bearing, more than proud.

Mass stood to the side of Rex, carrying a long, bejewelled spear. His clothing consisted of grey trunks and a leather shoulder band from which a knife hung.

Wolf, the last of the Thunderdogs, wore a long jacket, edged in gold, across a light blue tunic, with a gold belt around his waist from which hung a glimmeringly detailed sword.

The Thundercats took in all this detail, awed by the sheer glow and show of the group. Imperious Rex, a full half metre taller than Lion-O, stepped forward, his walk deliberate, powerful and graceful. He strode over, looking down on Lion-O.

"We saved these poor people from the demon threat — probably caused by that old sorcerer, Mumm-Ra, I reckon." Rex gave out a short, sneering laugh. "Didn't take long. Didn't take much effort. No sweat. No problem." he smiled chillingly at Lion-O. "Just as well we were around, really. Can't see you little kittens having managed it. Would've been bad for the Molemen."

Lion-O felt anger stirring, but tried to recover his composure.

"It's good you were around. You saved these people all right! Are you, uh, planning on staying around?" Rex smiled again. Lion-O really didn't like that smile.

"Well, we were certainly thinking about that, kitty-kitty." he scratched one fang with a short blade drawn from his waistband. "We were thinking how we were needed here, that maybe we'd stay a long time!" He let out a little chuckle. "So maybe you'd better think about, oh I don't know..." he looked skywards, then back down on Lion-O, grinning widely," ...how about *gardening?*"

Lion-O was fuming now. He turned away from Rex, afraid he might hit the Thunderdog. Rex was enjoying it.

"*Going* somewhere, kitty-kitty? Better rush, get in some gardening before sundown... get used to it. You aren't going to be doing much heroics from now on, eh? Not with *us* here!"

Panthro had had enough.

"Watch your tongue, butch! We've done quite enough to make ourselves welcome on this planet! Stopping one bunch of Mumm-Ra's demons isn't everything!"

Rex peered nastily at Panthro, who met his gaze equally. Neither flinched. Cheetara intervened before a fight broke out.

"Well, I'm sure I speak for us all in welcoming you to Third Earth and wishing you all the best here, Mr. Rex—"

"IMPERIOUS Rex, kitty," he sneered back. "You'll *soon* get used to the name."

Not another word was spoken. The Thundercats left, angry and confused. The Thunderdogs looked on, smug and grinning.

The next few weeks were some of the most miserable the Thundercats had ever spent. How could they object to other heroes? Lives were being saved all over the place, as Mumm-Ra stepped up his evil scheming, and one natural disaster after another kept happening. The Forest of Giant Insects had been overrun by a plague of Mutants. The Thunderdogs had been there to stop them. Berbil Village had almost fallen down a fissure created by an earthquake, but the heroic acts of Wolf and Imperious Rex had led to the sealing of the fissure. The Bridge of Light had flickered out. Cur found a way to recreate the mystical forces that powered it.

And so on.

And so on.

The Thundercats rose to every occasion, charged fearlessly in to solve every dilemma, each crisis, any disaster. Without fail, the Thunderdogs were either polishing off a marauding army, solving some mystical problem, or had already left, having done the job ages earlier. The Thundercats were beginning to feel foolish.

Lion-O, who only recently had spoken of a need for some peace, felt frustrated at getting his wish. The fact that the Thunderdogs were so good irritated him strangely. They were so smug, so self-important. But *good*. Really good.

"Why are they *always* there first?!" Lion-O cried out to no one in particular, waving his arms high. Tygra wasn't impressed with the young leader's outcry.

"Now wait a moment, Lion-O," he cautioned, "You can't change the fact that they've done good. Lots of it."

"Sure. Lots and lots and lots. Tons of it! They're so brimming with goodwill towards everybody, I'm surprised no-one's organised a parade while they take a breath between disasters!"

Tygra had his own reservations about the Thunderdogs. For now, he felt it was his duty to calm Lion-O.

"You're not a little... *jealous*, are you, Lion-O?"

Lion-O looked shocked. He hadn't even thought.

"I-no, of course not, it's just I..." Lion-O was confused. "They aren't what they seem!" He looked to Tygra for help.

"No. But that's not the point. We can't monopolise the 'good deeds' business, and getting irate with the Thunderdogs makes it look like we only do what we do for the glory." Tygra impressed himself by being so rational, though he'd have loved to have taught the overbearing Imperious Rex a lesson at their first meeting.

"I suppose you're right... but..." he didn't finish the sentence. It would have sounded so much like sour grapes to everyone else. He had suspicions, but no evidence. Yet.

The dramatic endeavours of the Thunderdogs continued. The many and various groups on the planet came to accept the Thunderdogs as the folk heroes of Third Earth. Several of the Thundercats began to wonder – were they needed anymore? Was it time to find another world? The Thunderdogs were certainly making it an uncomfortable place to be for a has-been group of heroes...

Around Cats' Lair, activities continued at a subdued pace. No one cared much about anything. Tygra got on with designing devices they would probably never use now that the occasions to outwit Mumm-Ra and his henchmen had gone. Panthro cleaned an already gleaming Thundertank, unused for weeks. Wilykat and Wilykit spent time with Cheetara learning more about the world of Thundera. Lion-O walked the corridors of Cats' Lair alone.

The greater the praise for the Thunderdogs, the worse Lion-O felt. He couldn't shake the feeling that something was very, very wrong.

Snarf had, for some time now, been aware of his young leader's sad moods. He watched him walk silent corridors, listened to him sigh at some unspoken thought. But what to do? Lion-O had kept to himself since his talk with Tygra. Snarf *had to* get him out of the doldrums...

"Ta da!"

Lion-O looked up from the exercise machine he had been working out on. Snarf was balancing upside down on one arm, juggling five berbilfruit between his feet, a massive, desperate grin glued to his face.

"I said – 'Ta da!' The amazing, wondrous Snarf is here to entertain, to illuminate, to—"

"I'm not in the mood, Snarf." Lion-O was offhand, weary.

Snarf got irate. "Listen, chuckles! It's taken ·me *hours* to get that trick right, *Snarf,* you might at least *look* at it!"

Lion-O only smiled wearily.

"Is it those Thunderdogs that've got you down, huh?" asked Snarf encouragingly. Lion-O shrugged. Snarf tried again. "Well, we don't need to bother with them, do we? We're the Thunder-thunder-THUNDERCATS!"

Snarf leapt into the air, arm raised as if holding up the Sword of Omens, and fell flat on his face. He looked up to see if Lion-O was laughing. He wasn't.

"I'm sorry, Snarf, I'm just not in the mood

right now." Snarf looked sadly at him, and started to leave. "Snarf," he turned, expectant. "... do you think I'd make a *good* gardener?"

The next day the alarm sounded in Cats' Lair. Wearily, Panthro looked up from polishing the Thundertank. The light blinked off, as it always did these days.

"Well, how about that. Emergency cancelled. I wonder who got there," said Panthro, already knowing the answer.

No one was surprised. No one did anything. It had become run of the the mill. No-one expected to see any action, and so no-one prepared to go out. Except one...

As the bell sounded, Snarf leapt up from the stool where he had been concocting that day's dinner and charged into the control room, picking up the monitor control. Cheetara, alarmed at the smoke pouring from the kitchen, ran in to find food burning furiously on the stove, and Snarf nowhere to be seen.

"Where could he have gone?" she asked herself, dousing the flames. Then she went back to the snooze she'd been in before the smoke had awoken her. The alarm hadn't disturbed her at all. She heard it too often. And it always stopped, anyway.

At the foot of Hook Mountain, in the Kingdom of the Snowmen, King Hanuman shook hands gratefully with Imperious Rex. Mumm-Ra had sent a horde of vicious Kleggosaur and Mubmub birds to attack the castle. Luckily, the Thunderdogs just happened to be passing on their way home from a party given in their honour at the Caves of Trolls and Giants, thanking them for protecting the land from the Phantasy Beasts of Glogshevva the previous week. It had been *no problem* to sort out the evil bird creatures.

"Think *nothing* of it, King Hanuman," said Rex in a mock-modest manner. "Me and the lads, we needed a bit of a workout after that food. Did us *all* good, eh?"

The king smiled.

"I don't know *what* we did before you came along—" he stopped, realising what he had said, instantly recalling the many times the Thundercats had saved them. "Er, I mean... that is, not to say the Thundercats didn't—"

Rex winked at the king. The Thunderdogs grinned. "Hey, Kingy, *we* get the picture, right, guys?"

There were mutters of agreement, and

small nasty laughs that alarmed the king. Rex became jovial again.

"Well, it's been really great helping you out like this, Hanny, but me and the lads have got other villains to beat, other disasters to quell, stuff like that. Remember" — Rex looked his most sincere — "I want you to call us anytime if there's the *slightest* disaster, calamity, upheaval, plague of frogomorphs, vast green flying things that go squark — *anytime* — OK? Remember our motto, Hanny — 'NO PROBLEM'. Saving folk is *our* business", he grinned again. "*Accept no substitutes,* right?"

N o Problem", muttered Snarf to himself, "no problem indeed..." He was hidden behind a snowbank watching the departing Thunderdogs. He'd arrived in time to hear Rex's nasty asides about the Thundercats. Had he been doing that every time he'd saved someone? Gradually making everyone believe that the Thundercats were a useless bunch of amateurs? The idea annoyed Snarf, who let out a small growl.

"*Grrsnarf!* I'll show them!" he said to himself. But show them what? He would have to think about it...

Snarf spent the rest of the day trailing the Thunderdogs. It was quite a day, too. The Kleggosaur and Mubmub birds staged two more assaults — luckily the Thunderdogs were on hand both times to see them off. In fact, it almost seemed to Snarf that maybe the Thunderdogs were there *before* the magical birds turned up.

Berbil Village suffered another earth tremor. The Thunderdogs dived in to save the day again, and Rex apologised for not having sorted things out properly last time the world cracked open. The Berbils were too grateful to complain.

Things slowed down a bit in the afternoon — a Bufflodrekker robot built by S-S-Slithe attacked the Treetop Village of the Warrior Women, its massive cyberhorns tearing at the bases of the trees. Snarl threw his weapons at the Bufflodrekker's mighty legs, smashing one, disabling another. Cur raised a blaster from under his cloak and blasted the nerve centre of the hulking robot, which just happened to be placed prominently between the two horns on its head. The robot stiffened, then fell over, just missing two more trees. The Thunderdogs were given garlands and gifts by the Warrior Women. Snarf, hidden behind a tree,

watched this — the *fifth* such victory that day — and found his suspicions growing.

As night began to fall, the Thunderdogs headed home, not knowing Snarf was still trailing them. Their home was a fort-type wood structure on the edge of the Swamp of Serpents. On top of each wall were razor-sharp tree trunks like massive, threatening pencils. To the other side was the Forest of Giant Insects. The Thunderdogs had settled there after they had beaten back the marauding Mutants a few weeks earlier. They could have had the pick of any site in Third Earth, so well were they regarded now. However, they chose to live in an inaccessible and frightening area. People assumed they had gone there to be ever-vigilant, not wanting to get as comfortable and lazy as (everyone now assumed) had the Thundercats.

That wasn't the reason.

It wasn't even *close*.

The Thunderdogs wanted to be away from the masses of Third Earth's residents.

Snarf was here to find out what the *real* reason was. His bravery astonished even himself. Here he was in one of the nastiest, creepiest parts of Third Earth, at night, even, and he hadn't whimpered or panicked at all. Well, not much. Certainly, the Thunderdogs hadn't noticed. They were too busy patting each other on the back and laughing at jokes that Snarf didn't fully understand. It seemed they didn't take being heroes all that seriously.

The Thunderdogs entered their fortress, passing under the sign proclaiming "THUNDERKENNEL: SUPERHEROES ONLY." Snarl and Cur were left on guard. Snarf looked for a way in, which meant climbing up one wall. He managed it, only falling off twice. From on top of the wall he could make out a barracks, with light shining out of the windows. The Thunderdogs' laughter could be heard. Snarf made his way down, peering through a window.

Rex was slouched back in a stout wooden chair, drinking from a large crystal tankard (a gift from the Rockmen for defeating the Cyber-Silicon Beast three weeks earlier). He and the other dogs, Mass, Brutus, and Wolf were finding something highly amusing. Snarf listened intently.

"...And — and then it came crashing down! WOOMP! S-S-Slithe *always* picks a great place to put those 'off' buttons! Ha ha ha!" laughed Rex. Wolf joined in:

"Re-hah hah-remember the —ha ha— Cosmo-Snake? —ha ha— and then Cur zapped it and —hahaha—" Wolf collapsed, laughing. Snarf was curious to hear the rest; the other three were wiping tears from their eyes at the reminder of this particular story. Wolf recovered enough to continue, "..An', an' it *fell over,* smashin' the wall of the castle! Hahahahaha!"

Snarf felt a surge of anger at the Thunderdogs' laughter. What kind of heroes were they, anyway? Suddenly, his attention was taken by a chilling voice from out of his field of view.

"You are smug, Rex. Don't make the mistake of overconfidence." Snarf tried to crane around and see who it was, but couldn't. "The Thundercats are frustrated that they are unable to do good deeds — but we want them *so* frustrated that they *leave* Third Earth!"

Snarf's eyes grew wider as he stifled a loud and whimpering 'Snarf' cry. The Thunderdogs were *deliberately* trying to get rid of them?!

"Yeah, well — we've been putting the word around like you said," Rex spoke to the figure Snarf still couldn't make out. "Making everyone believe those Thundercats are worse than useless — maybe we'll get them to think it themselves!" They all laughed at this. The figure moved tantalisingly close to Snarf's vision, but not enough to see him. He began to speak again:

"I want the Thundercats off this world. I want you to become the real heroes. There will be, of course, a *bonus* payment for this."

Rex grinned.

"Best money we've *ever* made as mercenaries, this is!" The others muttered their happy agreement. "Trade's been bad, but not now we're on contract with you, bandaged buddy!" The dogs all howled happily, banging their hands down on the table, stomping their feet. Snarf was appalled — 'bandaged buddy'? They couldn't mean—?

The figure stepped into view, sickly and savage. Master of all evil on Third Earth — First and Second Earth, come to that. MUMM-RA, THE EVER-LIVING!

Snarf couldn't hold it in any longer.

"*Snaaaaaarf!*" he held his hand over his mouth. Too late. The Thunderdogs super-sensitive hearing had caught the strangled whimper, and their braying laughter stopped abruptly.

Cur had Snarf by the arms before he could will his body to move from its fear-stricken pose.

Mumm-Ra tracked a decaying, withered finger across Snarf's face.

"Shame on you, little fuzzball. *Spying* on my brave heroes. You Thundercats must be so, *so* jealous", he sneered.

Snarf found courage from somewhere deep inside.

"They — *Snarf* — aren't heroes — *Snarf* — they just go where you *tell* them to go! You *create* all the disasters and monsters so that they can beat them and look *good!*"

Mumm-Ra might have smiled, but his expression was lost to Snarf in the incredible network of wrinkles.

"You *are* a clever little fuzzball", said Mumm-Ra. "What a *pity* you won't be able to *share* these thoughts with anyone..."

Snarf leapt up from the seat he had been placed on, grabbed the tankard and threw it at Mumm-Ra, who shattered it with a mystic bolt. The Thunderdogs ducked as shards of crystal flew all over the room. Snarf ran out.

"Rex! Earn your money!" raged Mumm-Ra. "Get that creature! Make sure it doesn't get away! FETCH!"

narf ran, panicking, tripping, stumbling through the trees. He didn't know where he was going and he didn't care, as long as it was away from the Thunderkennel. A break in the trees was ahead. He made for it, and looked out at the writhing mud of the Swamp of Serpents.

"Oh no... *Snarf*... oh no..." he muttered. A shadow, long and menacing, fell across Snarf who turned slowly, his face a mask of fear, as he looked up at the figure towering over him.

"Oh yes..." said Rex softly.

Snarf started to run, but tripped over a tree trunk, banging his head. He fell unconscious. Rex smiled widely. Lifting him up with one paw, he dropped Snarf into the mud. Snarf disappeared slowly under the surface of the swamp.

"No problem", said Rex, laughing nastily.

🐾 **CONTINUED ON PAGE 46** 🐾

THE CHRONICLES OF PLUN-DARR

And it came to pass that, on the nightside of Thundera's great sun, there turned an evil sister planet. The dark, blasted surface of **Plun-darr**, with its boiling oceans and scum deserts, played host to a vile race of pitiless, warmongering creatures — the **Evil Mutants**! Originally Plun-darr had been a sun-dappled paradise planet, surpassed in beauty only by Thundera. However, the Mutants had been at war with each other and the rest of the galaxy since the development of the spiked club some million winters earlier, and Plun-darr had long since begun to show signs of wear and tear. The Mutants' oldest enemies were the **Thunder-cats**, whose planet they had repeatedly tried to invade since plundering the secret of space travel from a crashed Dendrellian star-galleon. (It had been a flying Dendrellian star-galleon until it had entered Plun-daran airspace.) Time and again, **Warlord K-K-Komodo** of Plun-darr had launched major offensives against Thundera — and time and again the **Sword of Omens** had allowed the Thundercats to drive him back. It was rumoured that an **Eye of Plun-darr** had once existed — embedded in the hilt of the fabled **Scimitar of the Slain**, the Mutants' ancestral weapon of conquest. Legend told that the Scimitar lay somewhere in the caverns beneath **Darkenheath** in the **Mountains of Misery**, Plun-darr's capital city. But Darkenheath had been an unhabitable zone of lethal radioacivity since the Dendrellians extracted terrible revenge from Plun-darr for the shooting down of their star-galleon. The Scimitar of the Slain, it seemed, was lost forever, along with K-K-Komodo's reputation as a leader of Mutants. To replace him came **S-S-Slithe**, star graduate of Reptilian School and Evil University, and son of Ri-Kaxtr the Unspeakable. S-S-Slithe's plan was to steal the Sword of Omens — and, with it, the power of the Eye of Thundera. Plun-darr's scientists had predicted years earlier that both Plun-darr and Thundera would be destroyed in the changing orbit of their sun — and it was S-S-Slithe who led the **Mutant Ark Fleet**, including arch-henchmen **Monkian** and **Jackal-man** in pursuit of the Thundercats — to **Third Earth!**'

Illustration: **COLLINS/BASKERVILLE** Colour: **EUAN PETERS**

22

OH NO! THE FOREST IS ABLAZE! AND THAT MEANS THAT THE *TREETOP KINGDOM* OF THE *WARRIOR MAIDENS* IS *DOOMED!*

THE FIREBALLS OF PLUN-DARR!

Script **CRAIG ANDERSON** ● Pencils **ERNIE COLON** ● Inks **AL WILLIAMSON** ● Letters **PAT BROSSEAU** ● Colour **STUART PLACE**

THERE'S NO TIME TO SUMMON THE THUNDERCATS! THE WARRIOR MAIDENS HAVE HELPED US MANY TIMES IN THE PAST. I ONLY HOPE THAT I AM NOT TOO--

--LATE!

THUD!

OOF!

ON YOUR FEET, VILLAIN!

PREPARE TO-- TYGRA!

WILLA! WHAT THE DEVIL WAS THAT FOR?

I'M SORRY. THE BOMBARDMENT BEGAN BEFORE DAWN! TREES THAT HAVE LIVED A MILLION YEARS HAVE BEEN DESTROYED WITHIN HOURS! I'VE BEEN CHASING SHADOWS ALL DAY...

LOOK OUT!

RRAAOOUGH

IT'S MONKIAN, ONE OF S-S-SLITHE'S HENCHMEN! I MIGHT'VE KNOWN S-S-SLITHE WAS BEHIND THIS!

YA HAH HAH! I'M GONNA MOW YOU DOWN LIKE A BLADE OF GRASS!

WHACK

HE'LL GET US NEXT TIME UNLESS *I*--

YAAH! NO FAIR!

...GROUND *HIM!*

HELLLP

IT DIDN'T CRASH!

NO. IT PROBABLY HAS A REMOTE GUIDANCE SYSTEM.

RROOUGH

LISTEN! THE BOMBARDMENT'S STOPPED!

FOR NOW. OUR WORLD HAS CHANGED SINCE YOU AND THE MUTANTS ARRIVED. WE WARRIOR WOMEN HAVE BEEN CAUGHT IN THE MIDDLE OF YOUR BATTLES.

WE ARE BEING *DESTROYED!*

THERE'S STILL A CHANCE TO SAVE YOUR FOREST. WE MUST TAKE THE BATTLE TO THE SOURCE OF THE FIRE BOMB ATTACKS! TOGETHER WE'LL STRIKE THAT FORTRESS OF EVIL-- --CASTLE PLUN-DARR!

WHILE BACK AT THE CATS LAIR...

NO, LION-O! STOP!

YOU CAN'T LEAVE THE GAME JUST BECAUSE I'M WINNING!

IT'S NOT THAT, SNARF. SOMETHING'S WRONG. I CAN'T CONCENTRA--

WHERE'S TYGRA?

ON A MISSION SCOUTING NEW DEVELOPMENTS WITH THE MUTANT WAR MACHINES!

WE KNOW THEY'VE PUT TOGETHER TWO VEHICLES FROM PIECES OF THEIR WRECKED SPACESHIP.

IF THEY MAKE ANY MORE VEHICLES, THEY'LL PROBABLY ATTACK!

TYGRA'S INVISIBILITY MAKES HIM THE BEST THUNDERCAT FOR A MISSION LIKE THAT, PANTHRO, BUT...

...HE SHOULDN'T HAVE GONE ALONE!

CASTLE PLUN-DARR...

THE MUTANTS ARE USING SOME TYPE OF MACHINE TO LAUNCH GREAT BALLS OF LIQUID FIRE!

TYGRA, LOOK OUT!

THAT FIREBALL IS COMING STRAIGHT AT US!

WHOOSH

26

WE BARELY MADE IT!

BA-DOOM!

WE STILL HAVE TO GET PAST THAT MOAT.

YOUR BOLO WON'T HELP US THIS TIME. WE'LL HAVE TO SWIM!

NOT "WE," WILLA. *ME.*

SO WHY SHOULD I STAY, AND NOT YOU?

BECAUSE I HAVE THE BOLO! AND WITH IT, I CAN DO...

...*THIS!*

CRACKLE!

IN THE WATER! I'M *INVISIBLE,* WILLA! NOW I CAN SWIM ACROSS THE MOAT UNDETECTED!

TYGRA! WHERE ARE YOU?

WAIT A MINUTE! I THOUGHT YOU WERE AFRAID OF THE WATER!

AFTER A RUN-IN I HAD WITH SAFARI JO,* I THOUGHT I'D BETTER LEARN HOW TO SWIM!

*SEEN IN *THUNDERCATS WEEKLY* ISSUES 26 AND 27.

DID YOU SEE THAT? THERE WAS A BLUE FLASH, DOWN THERE, JUST ACROSS THE MOAT!

AAH, IT WAS PROBABLY JUST A SPARK FROM THE FIREBALL.

29

UH-OH! S-S-SLITHE IS COMING RIGHT *AT* ME! IF I DON'T FIND THE OPENING FAST--

CHAKA CHAKA

MAYBE THIS LOOSE ROCK?!

WOBBLE

UGH!!

CHEW ON THIS, MUTANT FIEND!

RRRRR

HEY! WHAT'S HAPPENING?!

WELL, THAT'S *ONE* THREAT OUT OF THE WAY, AND--

NO, IT CAN'T--BLUB BLABUB BLUB RUBA DUB!

KLANK BANG

THERE'S THE INTAKE PIPE! MY LUCK IS WITH ME!

UNFORTUNATELY FOR TYGRA IT'S *BAD* LUCK!

SNIKK!

31

TIME TO DRY OUT, THUNDERCATFISH! HEH HEH!

CLACK

THIS LEVER CONTROLS THE FOUR SEPARATE SPRING-LOADED CATAPULTS. IT'S VERY SENSITIVE!

SNOK

GRRRRR!

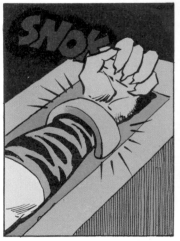

SNOK

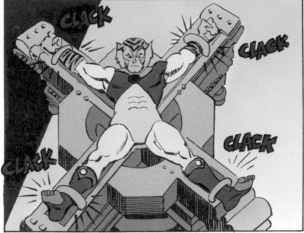

CLACK CLACK CLACK CLACK

NOW, THIS SOLAR MIRROR WILL TRIGGER THE CATAPULTS!

INGENIOUS, EH?

WITH THE FIRST RAYS OF THE SUN, YOU WILL STRETCH TILL YOU SNAP! HAHAHAHA!

33

34

THE EYE OF THUNDERA -- IT'S OPEN! B-BUT THAT MUST MEAN-- OH MY!

WE WON'T KNOW *WHAT* IT MEANS UNTIL I LOOK!

OH, LION-O, PLEASE DON'T SEE ANYTHING B-BAD!

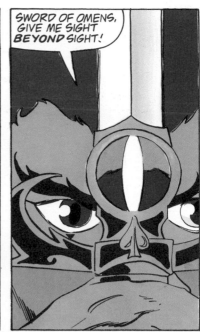

SWORD OF OMENS, GIVE ME SIGHT *BEYOND* SIGHT!

RRRRRR

LION-OOO

TYGRA! I'M COMING!

LION-O! WAIT! WHAT'S THE MATTER? DID YOU SEE TYGRA?

TELL ME!

LION-O, WHAT'D YOU SEE?

DON'T GO! PLEASE!

LION-O, DON'T GO...

LION-O RUNS TO THE MARSH WITHOUT HESITATION. BUT ONE SHOULD NOT RACE BLINDLY INTO DANGER...

YAA!

FOOM!

35

LION-O! I HAD A *FEELING* A THUNDERCAT WOULD COME SOON!

AND JUST IN TIME, TOO! I WAS ALL SET TO GO IN... *ALONE!*

WHERE'S TYGRA?

TYGRA SWAM TO CASTLE PLUN-DARR IN THE DARK. HE--

TYGRA *SWAM?*

I WAS SURPRISED TOO. HE WAS INVISIBLE. AFTER HE LEFT, I HEARD THE MOST FRIGHTENING SOUNDS COMING FROM THE MOAT--

ANOTHER MOAT?.

THIS MOAT. I FOUND TYGRA'S BOLO WHIP FLOATING IN IT.

WILLA, WE HAVE TO CROSS FAST! TYGRA IS IN DANGER! I KNOW IT!

"I SPIED AN OUTCROPPING ON THE CASTLE BASE. WE'LL HAVE TO RACE ACROSS BECAUSE...

"...DAWN HAS BROKEN!"

AT LEAST IT'S A BEAUTIFUL SUNRISE! I'M GLAD S-S-SLITHE AND HIS CRONIES DIDN'T STICK AROUND--THEY LEFT FOR BREAKFAST!

OUTSIDE...

NO-ONE'S SOUNDING THE ALARM! WE HAVEN'T BEEN SEEN YET!

BUT NOW WE HAVE TO SCALE THIS WALL! FORTUNATELY, I HAVE MY GLOVE-CLAW--

MY GLOVE-CLAW! IT'S GONE! I WAS IN SUCH A HURRY TO HELP TYGRA, THAT I FORGOT IT AS I LEFT CATS' LAIR!

NEVER MIND, LION-O. WE'RE GOING TO HAVE SOME HELP!

COME ON! WAKE UP! TIME FOR SOME WORK!

LION-O, MEET BUSHY. IT'S A TREETOP SPIDER. ISN'T IT *CUTE?!*

37

40

THE FIREBALL LAUNCHER--BUILT FROM THE *PROPULSION UNIT* OF THE MUTANTS' WRECKED SPACE VEHICLE!

THAT TANK MUST CONTAIN THE *FUEL.*

THIS IS WHAT THEY USED TO DESTROY MY TREETOP KINGDOM!

AND THEY'LL USE IT AGAIN TO DESTROY THE CATS' LAIR--

UNLESS WE *DESTROY IT FIRST!*

NO! NO! NO!

THEY'RE *INSIDE!!* AND THEY'VE *LOCKED* THE DOOR!

MELT IT DOWN! HURRY, YOU FOOL!

PUFF PUFF

NOT TO WORRY, S-S-SLITHE! I'LL HAVE THIS DOOR *MELTED* IN A JIFFY!

HURRY! HURRY! HURRY!

HERE'S A SIMPLE SOLUTION TO A COMPLEX PROBLEM!

BUT THERE'S A *CATCH--SOMEONE* HAS TO STAY AND LIGHT THIS THING...

...BUT HOW WILL HE GET OUT BEFORE IT GOES OFF?

DO YOU *SMELL* SOMETHING?

THUNDER-*THUNDER*-THUNDER-

THUNDERCATS HO!

41

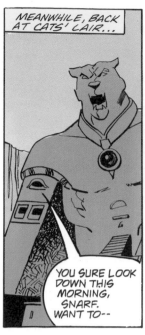

MEANWHILE, BACK AT CATS' LAIR...

YOU SURE LOOK DOWN THIS MORNING, SNARF. WANT TO--

EH, WHAT'S THIS? LION-O'S CLAW--

--GLOVE. HE LEFT SO FAST, HE FORGOT IT. I HOPE HE DOESN'T NEED IT.

A BURDEN LIKE THAT SHOULD NOT BE CARRIED ALONE, SNARF. AND LOOK THERE! YOUR WAIT IS OVER!

LET'S GET INTO THE THUNDER-TANK!

PANTHRO READY-- HO!

CHEETARA READY-- HO!

WILYKIT AND KAT READY-- HO!

SNARF =GRUNT= READY-- HO!

WHILE...

THEY'LL BE HERE IN A MINUTE!

QUICK! STAND BACK-TO-BACK! WE'LL GIVE THEM A FIGHT THAT WILL LIVE ON IN LEGEND!

THERE'S THE THUNDERTANK! THE THUNDERCATS' ARE HERE!

THUNDERCATS, HO!!

VRRMM!

42

43

THE CHRONICLES OF THIRD EARTH

And it came to pass that the noblecats of **Thundera** and the Mutants of **Plun-darr** did make planetfall on a small blue-green planet, third in line from a young and vital sun. **Third Earth** was already home to a great variety of races and species, some of whom welcomed the alien newcomers, and some of whom did not. One such was **Mumm-Ra the Ever Living**, ancient devil priest and former ruler of Third Earth. A thousand years before the arrival of the Thundercats, Mumm-Ra ruled the world as **Pharoah Ka-Rey-Bar**, from the luxury of a great **Onyx Pyramid**

However, Ka-Rey-Bar was merely a front for Mumm-Ra's true activities, and his was a five-hundred year reign of terror. It ended with the great **Rammastide** uprising, in which the oppressed peoples of Third Earth banded together against their cruel ruler. Powerful though he was, Mumm-Ra could not withstand the combined threat of his angry subjects, and the fierce struggle which followed could have only one conclusion. Hopelessly outnumbered, Mumm-Ra and his **Thugron** armies were driven back to the Onyx Pyramid. There the devil priest still waits, his now ancient body swathed in life-giving bandages. Although able to summon the ancient forces in short bursts, to restore his youth and vigour, Mumm-Ra cannot maintain the level for long, and now relies on cunning and deceit to carry out his evil plans. The arrival of the Thundercats on Third Earth held the promise of a new lease of life, when Mumm-Ra discovered that the Thunderian Flagship, carrying Lion-O and his fellow 'Cats to the planet, also bore the **Eye of Thundera**, mystic crystal of time — lost power. Mumm-Ra was joined in his pursuit of the Eye by Reptilian **S-S-Slithe** of the **Evil Mutants**, and both formed an uneasy alliance in their aim to outwit and destroy the 'Cats. There might be some small dispute over ownership of the Eye after it came into their possession — but neither S-S-Slithe nor Mumm-Ra are worried. After all, they never *really* trusted one another...'

Illustration: **COLLINS/BASKERVILLE** Colour: **EUAN PETERS**

45

THUNDERDOGS HO! PART 2

Plot **SIMON FURMAN** ● Story **MIKE COLLINS** ● Illustrations **DARREN GOODACRE** ● Colour **STEVE WHITE**

he next day dawned. The Thundercats went about their business. Cheetara went to the natural springs on the banks of the River of Despair to fill pitchers, as Snarf was not around to do it. No-one had seen him since the previous morning, but weren't too worried — after all, if he couldn't look after himself in a situation, the Thunderdogs could always see to him, couldn't they?

This did not particularly concern Cheetara as she carried out the morning chores. She hummed to herself a song she had been teaching Wilykat and Wilykit the previous day. It was all about the lava forests and emerald fountains of Thundera, and how rainbows glowed in each green crystal, and how the lava shimmered in the noonday sun... of the soft feather meadows, the

gentle singing rains... she began to feel melancholy. She had decided that today was the day she would broach the subject of leaving Third Earth. The others would understand. She sensed they felt the same. No one seemed to want them here any more.

"What's *that*?" she suddenly said out loud. A strange shape was visible in the river. It drifted by her position. She put down the pitchers, and followed it as it came to rest on the riverbank some metres down.

She walked towards it slowly, cautiously. Cheetara had long since recognised it. She didn't want to believe her eyes, though. Up close, she had no choice.

"Snarf!" she cried out. She ran to his barely-breathing figure, covered in the muck and mire of the river. She held his body, his barely-beating heart a vague sound to her keen ears. "Oh, Snarf..."

She was back at the Cats' Lair in record time.

Panthro examined Snarf for some time. The other Thundercats said nothing, not wishing even to think about what could and had happened to Snarf. Eventually Panthro, head bowed, came out of the room in which they had placed their small friend.

"How is he? Is he — going to be... all right?"

Panthro, with a sad expression, only shrugged. Lion-O barged past him and knelt by Snarf's bed. Tears were not far from his eyes.

"Oh, Snarf... where did you go? *Why* did you go? Who did this...?" He gritted his teeth, held back his tears and turned to the others. "Someone will pay for this! And I know who!"

Lion-O stood up, hand reaching down for his sword. Tygra's hand rested gently on his.

"Lion-O, those are words of anger and desperation. We don't know that *anyone* did this to Snarf. Accidents will happen..." Tygra looked to Lion-O who looked anxious, confused.

"You don't want to hear it, do you?" said Lion-O. "I *told* you those Thunderdogs were no good —" Tygra stopped him.

"You don't know that the Thunderdogs had *anything* to do with this. You have no proof. You disliked that Imperious Rex when you first met him — you can't blame him for everything —" Lion-O pushed past Tygra, his face a mask of anger and pain.

"I'm not a cub anymore. I *know* I'm right!" The others watched him go, silent.

No-one saw Lion-O for several hours. He had gone to his room to be with his toys — the precious few mementoes of a childhood he had missed in fleeing Thundera. He had spent those lonely hours thinking about Snarf, how he had looked after Lion-O; how Lion-O had made fun of him; how they had meant so much to each other. *Do* mean to each other, Lion-O corrected himself. He *will* pull through...

Lion-O got up from the bed where he had lain. He put the toys to one side. He strapped to his waist the belt from which hung the Sword of Omens, symbol of his grown-up life.

He had work to do.

Panthro was in the Cats' Lair lab , working on a sample of the mud that Snarf had been

covered in. He turned to find Lion-O standing behind him.

"Well?" asked Lion-O curtly. "What have you found?"

Panthro held a slide up to the light, examining it.

"Remember — these are only initial results... not conclusive..." He looked away from the slide and at Lion-O. "So don't go jumping to conclusions."

Lion-O raised an eyebrow, pupils dilated. Panthro began to feel uncomfortable.

"Well?" repeated Lion-O.

"The mud actually seems to have come from the Swamp of Serpents. Now, there must be some outlet from the Swamp to the River of Despair... Snarf was lucky the Serpents didn't find him tasty enough to bite. Why he would have been near the Swamp is beyond me — what's up there besides..." He stopped and looked around. The room was empty. Quietly he finished his sentence, "...the Thunderdogs' Fortress..."

Imperious Rex was leading a weapons practice and keep-fit session for the Thunderdogs at the Thunderkennel. S-S-Slithe had got into the swing of creating bigger and more bizarre robots for the Thunderdogs to defeat, and Mumm-Ra had promised that today's would be a real spectacle.

Just after noon, an enormous four-winged Rimmersaurus Spektikus with detachable Monothreat Vampiroid Bats was to attack the Treetop Kingdom of Willa and the Warrior Women in revenge for the defeat of the Bufflodrekker. The 'off' switch was situated under the rear left wing of the Rimmersaurus. Cur's 'blaster' was really a remote control device. Aim it, and the robot would give a satisfying 'boom' noise. To add to the spectacle this time, the Monothreat Vampiroids would also explode, creating a dramatic and dazzling firework display, visible for several kilometres around. The crowning event in the Thunderdogs' long campaign.

However, an event of such importance deserved a first-rate show; some swinging from vines hung from the treetop homes, death-defying leaps, and so forth. All this required the correct preparation, which is what Rex and the Thunderdogs were doing as the vast gates of the Thunderkennel were smashed to matchwood by the rapid slashes of a sword.

"And a one — two — zap that bird, and a

three — four —"

CRASH! SLASH! BANG!

"Who's at the door?!" All the Thunderdogs turned, shocked to see their mighty doors shattered in tiny pieces around the feet of the rage-filled Lion-O.

Imperious Rex drew himself up to his full height and walked over to Lion-O.

"Well, well. Kitty-kitty has come to see the heroes at play, has he?"

Lion-O was too angry to speak. He gritted his teeth, letting out a low growl.

"You know, kitty — you only had to *knock*. We'd have let you in. . ." Rex patted Lion-O on the head, grinning at the angry Thundercat. Lion-O snatched himself away, and Mass, Wolf and Cur took their opportunity for a *real* fight. They were tired of play-acting. They were mercenaries, not actors. They didn't want to be stage-managed. They wanted to fight.

The three charged at Lion-O.

"Mess with our leader, would you, puddy-cat?!" yelled Wolf with a little more glee than righteous anger. Weapons out, the three attacked him.

The fight was over in no time — though Lion-O could have picked off each of them individually, none were fighting fair and he was overwhelmed. Lion-O realised that he was holding back as well — after all, hadn't Panthro *told* him he shouldn't jump to conclusions? Wasn't that exactly what he *had* done?

In Lion-O's doubt-filled confusion, Wolf was able to wrest the Sword of Omens from him. Lion-O managed to send him flying, but got hit on the head by Mass's bejewelled spear. Pain shot up one leg as Lion-O realised that Wolf was back, and was trying to bite his ankle. Falling back, Lion-O found himself pinned to the ground, as Cur went to his throat with a knife.

Cur suddenly vanished from Lion-O's chest, as much a surprise to him as to Lion-O. Rex held him suspended in mid-air by his collar. Cur grinned sheepishly at his leader. Rex ignored him, and proceeded to be polite to Lion-O, who was attempting to get up, as Wolf and Mass backed off.

"I'd like to apologise for the. . . over-eager behaviour of my aides. They saw you manhandle me, so they feared the worst. After all, you did do *that* —" he pointed to the shattered gate, "didn't you, kitty?"

What could Lion-O say? He had blundered in — had the Thunderdogs attacked the Lair, would he have done anything

different? And Imperious Rex *was* apologising. . .

"I'm sorry — I was just. . . upset", said Lion-O weakly.

Rex shrugged. "I go for long walks, read a bit of poetry when I'm depressed. I'll have to try smashing a door to pieces. See if it does anything for me." He dusted Lion-O off, still talking in a pleasant manner. "What caused this depression then? Gardening turning out to be a tougher deal than you thought? Missing out on the glory? Someone kicked sand in your face? Can't get the regular brand of kitty litter at the local store anymore?" His tone was becoming gradually more unpleasant. Lion-O felt he was being made fun of. He wanted to leave. Oh, why had he even come here?

That's why, he suddenly thought. Snarf. His resolve came back, instantly.

"I was upset because a friend of mine had an accident."

Rex suddenly stiffened. He looked around, then back at Lion-O.

"One of the kiddies fall off their skyboards? The ladycat trip on her staff?" Rex's lines were meant to be humorous, but he sounded worried. *Could* he have done something to Snarf?

"Snarf. He fell into the Swamp of Serpents.

Do you know anything about that, Imperious Rex?"

"He's the one with the big ears? No, can't say I've seen him... but that there Swamp is a bad place to wander by. Anything could happen. Anyone could fall in. Even I've slipped on the banks around there. Send my *best* wishes. He's not *said* anything, then?"

"Nothing. He hasn't come round yet." Lion-O was so unsure. Was he being lied to or not?

"I think I speak for all the lads when I say," Rex looked around, an expression of mock grief on his face, "— that we really hope the little critter doesn't suffer much longer. That he gets better, that is."

Lion O felt himself hopelessly outclassed.

"Listen, about your gate," he said. "It won't take me long to get another built... let me pay... I have to apologise—"

"Grant that hound no words of regret, Lion-O!" At the sound of the voice, all heads turned. It was Tygra and the other Thunder-cats, standing in the shattered doorway. They all looked grim.

Cur started to slink away, but Rex grabbed him by the collar.

"Oh boy," said Cur, "we are truly for it now, and that's no lie..."

Tygra pointed at Rex, who visibly wilted.

"Snarf came to just after Lion-O left. He was conscious long enough to tell us what you did to him. All the details. Thunderdogs-*Ha*!"

Lion-O looked outraged at this news. Rex tried a weak smile.

"Now — don't go judging us without all the facts —"

"The game is up, you fool! The pretence will no longer work! Just get rid of them!" It was Mumm-Ra who had mystically appeared, right next to Rex. Rex looked as if a great weight had been lifted from his shoulders.

"You mean — stomping time? Rrrright! NO PROBLEM!" Rex grinned widely, drew his sword from his back. "Thunderdogs — STOMP!"

The two sides launched into each other, and the fight began in earnest. Panthro charged at Imperious Rex, knocking him down.

"I've been waiting to do that!" he said.

Rex got up and sent him flying. Cur and Mass both went at Cheetara, weapons swinging wildly. Neither knew about her swiftness, and collided with each other as she zipped between them.

umm-Ra took his spirit form back to the Onyx Pyramid, to watch the battle in safety. He was grim faced about the matter.

"They are so well balanced", he cursed. "The Thundercats may possibly win...unless I can alter the situation, so that *my* side has the advantage... heh heh..."

He made the image of the fight disappear from the flames of his cauldron and called up the image of his servant, S-S-Slithe...

he battle continued, going badly for the Thundercats. Mass, having swiftly recovered from crashing into Cur, had brought down Tygra, hitting him from behind. Using Tygra as a shield he had launched an attack on Lion-O, knowing that Lion-O wouldn't hurt his friend. Lion-O was confused as to what to do, trying to parry past Tygra's unconscious form.

Rex had Cheetara by the hair, and lifted her up, his grin showing all his vicious-looking teeth.

"You think *this* is painful, kitty lady? Just you... wa-arrrgh!" He dropped Cheetara

and started hopping around, holding the foot that Wilykit had just jumped on.

"I may be small, but I can get myself noticed!" She leapt back on her board and flew out of his reach. Cheetara took the opportunity to extend her staff and start hitting Rex with it.

"Ow! Ow! Ow!" the big Thunderdog bellowed.

Panthro came to with Wolf crouched over him.

"We're not going to be any trouble now, *are* we?" said the gleeful Wolf, knife out and near Panthro's face.

Wolf raised his knife arm, heard a *swoosh*, but ignored it. He came to bring the knife back down, and found his hand empty.

"Uh-oh..." He looked at Panthro, who was now smiling. He looked around to see Wilykat holding his knife just out of reach on his skyboard. He looked back at Panthro. "Uh-oh..."

WHAKK!

Panthro lifted the now unconscious Wolf off him and joined the others in battle.

Tygra came round to see Lion-O standing in front of him, swinging a sword. Why? Tygra looked down and saw he'd grown a third arm, and was fighting Lion-O back with his sword. After a second his mind cleared. Someone — the owner of the arm — was using him a shield.

WHOK! Tygra lowered the unconscious Cur gently to the ground.

The battle was definitely going the Thundercats' way. Luckily for the 'Dogs, a massive cloud seemed to pass over the battle. They all looked up, the battle forgotten for a moment.

"What a *wonderful* Rimmersaurus Spektikus," Rex said to himself. Several smaller figures, barely visible in the bright sun, flew from the great metal bird. "And what delightful detachable Monothreat Vampiroid Bats..."

The Thundercats ducked for cover as the Vampiroids attacked. Rex and the Dogs reclaimed their fallen weapons. Lion-O managed to cut through four of the bats as they launched themselves at him, before he fell. Wilykat and Wilykit found themselves smothered by the birds, no more than a metre wingspan each and, unable to control their boards, they crashed to the ground.

Cheetara found herself lifted into the air as the bats grabbed either end of her staff. They just as swiftly let her drop. Her fall was broken by Panthro, and both were knocked

out. Tygra fell before too long at the onslaught.

Luckily for the 'Dogs.

The Thundercats came to, finding themselves restrained, all roped up. Looking up, they saw the fortress tops had the mechanical bats perched on them, looking down on the scene. Over the entrance, the Rimmersaurus had perched itself, all four wings wrapped around itself.

Imperious Rex and the other Thunderdogs also looked down on the Thundercats, satisfied grins on all faces.

"Well, the kitties have come around! Our pals came in at the right time, eh? Maybe we could give them a job, huh? The 'Thunderbats', eh?" said Rex.

The other 'Dogs laughed heartily at their leader's joke. He turned to look at them, one fang jutting out from his mouth, his eyebrows raised.

"OK, OK, it wasn't *that* funny." They promptly stopped.

Lion-O snarled at Rex.

"What are you going to do with us now then, Rex? You can't let us go, can you? We might ruin your goody-goody image."

Rex looked hurt, then smiled. Lion-O was

beginning to wish he wouldn't do that. There was never a nice result.

"You hurt me, kitty-kitty. Do you think anyone is going to believe any story you sourpuss pussy cats tell about us? Hmm. Maybe you *are* right. Some just might. Ungrateful bunch. And after all we've done for them, too." He seemed to be thinking. "But, being the great guy I am, I think we *will* let you go."

The Thundercats looked both surprised and suspiscious.

"You think this is all a joke, don't you?" Tygra growled, struggling with his ropes. "Wait until I'm free, I'll show you. . ."

Rex waved one hand at him dismissively.

"They're magic ropes, courtesy of our bandaged buddy. But I'm not joking, you know – You *are* going –" he pointed over to the left of the compound where Cur and Mass were pulling off a canopy from something. "You are going – in that!"

It was a space cruiser, battered from battles between planets. On one side was painted the craft's name: 'STAR ROVER', and a grinning dog's head, all teeth showing. In large letters across the front was their motto: 'NO PROBLEM'.

Wolf went inside and started the engines up.

Rex turned back to the Cats and carried on explaining, telling then the story he would tell all of Third Earth. . .

"You see, the battle with the robot birds became so intense, you Thundercats ended up showing your true colours and fled in panic. You broke into our compound –" he indicated the door, "as anyone could see, and went off in our ship, hoping to return when *we* had polished off the birds, but," he grinned yet again, "and this is the *tragic* bit. . ." he wiped away an imaginary tear, "we couldn't stop you in time to tell you the ship's guidance systems were set for deepest space and couldn't be changed." He thumped his chest with one paw. "Gets you right here, don't it?"

Panthro struggled with his bonds, yelling at Rex.

"No one will believe that rubbish!"

"With you kitties off the planet, it won't really matter what *anyone* believes, will it?" Rex took out his short knife and began scratching his fang with it. "We will be here – forever – and so long as our bandaged buddy pays, we'll keep order on his terms."

Booming sounds could be heard from the ship as the engines fired up.

"Soon be ready," said Cur, who ran over from the ship. "Wolf is getting everything going." Rex smiled at Cur, who looked pathetically grateful.

"I hope none of you gets space-sick" said Rex, walking away from the Thundercats.

"What can we do?" asked Wilykat, looking as worried as the rest.

"I have an idea," said Lion-O, musing to himself. He looked to where their weapons were dumped, close by. "Wilykat – try to shuffle over while they're all concentrating on the spaceship. Shuffle over to the weapons pile, and drag the Sword of Omens to me."

"What good will that do? They'll be back before you've even begun cutting through the magic bonds" said Wilykat unhappily.

Lion-O grinned at him. "Unless they were distracted by something, eh?"

"What have you in mind, young cub?" asked Tygra, confused.

Lion-O winked. "Wait and see."

Wilykat shuffled over, his hands tied behind his back, to the weapons pile, awkwardly grabbing the Sword of Omens. The Thunderdogs were all by the ship and paid him no attention.

He dragged the sword back to Lion-O.

"Hold it in front of me," whispered Lion-O. Wilykat did. Lion-O pressed his forehead to it. "Give me sight *beyond* sight!" he whispered. He then saw the way the Rimmersaurus worked, and what hitting the 'off' button would do.

"That should be diversion enough", he said to himself. "Wilykat, point the sword at that red area under the big bird's wing. Activate the light beam in the sword."

Wilykat, not understanding, followed the order. The beam caught S-S-Slithe's secret switch.

WHAKOOOOOOM! VADOOOOM! ZAKROOOOM! BADOOM! BADOOOM!

The whole top of the fortress was lit up by explosions. The automatic circuit had worked brilliantly. All the bats went up when the big bird exploded. It could be seen for kilometres around. People came rushing from all over. In the confusion, Lion-O had the chance to cut through all the Thundercats' bonds.

The 'Dogs had been running around in confusion, believing they were being attacked. Rex yelled for them to calm down, but they were all well past reason.

"Stop! It's only the birds! STOP!" He stopped yelling as he felt a hand reaching up to tap him on the shoulder from behind.

He turned to look at the Thundercats, fully armed, standing there.

"Uh-oh," he said.

People were charging into the stockade, confusion was everywhere.

"I can explain EVERYTHING!" yelled Rex, trying to get control of the situation. Everyone looked at him. "THEY did all this!" He pointed at the Thundercats. More bats exploded on a delayed circuit which S-S-Slithe had put in as an afterthought, to be more dramatic. People started running around again. Lion-O walked calmly up to Rex, who was looking around him, as people darted around in panic. The sharpened tops of the stockade were now aflame.

"I thought you were going to explain everything," Lion-O said in a conversational tone. "Why did you have S-S-Slithe's machines around your fortress? Why were we tied up when everyone started running in? Why is Wolf firing up your ship?"

Lion-O was enjoying the reversal of the situation. Imperious Rex knew their time was up. He shouted to his 'Dogs, who were now milling about in panic like everyone else.

"THUNDERDOGS! To the STAR ROVER! *ABANDON PLANET!*"

The dogs all ran for the ship, barging past the Third Earth residents, who were totally lost as to what was going on.

The STAR ROVER shot off from the planet's surface with a thunderous roar, and was in space in seconds. The Thundercats watched it go. A confused Warrior Woman approached Lion-O.

"We and the Snowmen had come to thank the Thunderdogs for what they had done for us yesterday," she said. "Did they blow up their fortress and go away? Who will protect us now?!"

Lion-O smiled.

"Well, I suppose you'll have to make do with us again!" She looked surprised.

"But all these disasters — how will you cope?"

"Oh, I think they'll stop being *quite* so dramatic now..."

veryone left the area around the fortress. The Thunderkennel was no more. Panthro looked up, remembered something, and turned to Tygra.

"Do you suppose... do you suppose maybe they thought to alter the navigation computers' instructions to go flying into deepest space?"

The two looked at each other, and burst out laughing.

he Thundercats started on the long march back to Cats' Lair. Tygra walked with Lion-O.

"How is Snarf then?" asked Lion-O.

"We can't be sure. We'll know more when he regains consciousness."

Lion-O looked startled at this information.

"But you said he *had*—"

Tygra stopped him.

"We guessed you had come here. That left us with a simple choice — believe your instincts, or believe in the character of six highly dubious 'heroes' I never believed in from the start."

"You lied, then?" Lion-O was startled.

"Well, not quite. After all, I never actually *said* what the truth about the Thunderdogs was, did I? I didn't know! Rex just *reacted* as though I knew. Never break the moral code of a Thundercat, Lion-O. Maybe sometimes *bend* it a little, as circumstances dictate..."

"Well, at least we won't be seeing them again." Lion-O paused. "Snarf *is* going to be all right, isn't he?"

Tygra winked.

"NO PROBLEM!"

THUNDERCATS™

PAST PERILS TIMES TWO!

PART 2.

DAYBREAK ON *FIRST EARTH*. WITH THE DAWN COMES *LION-O*, AND AN ODD ASSORTMENT OF COMPANIONS...

...LEADING THE ASSAULT ON THE INCOMPLETE *ONYX PYRAMID* OF *MUMM-RA*!

Script **MIKE COLLINS** ● Pencils **ANDY WILDMAN** ● Inks **DAVE HINE** ● Letters **GLIB** ● Colour **LOUISE CASSELL**

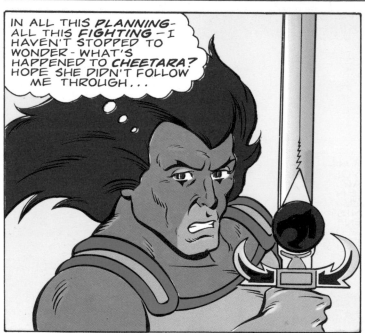

AGAIN? I FEAR THE *DESERT SUN* HAS AFFECTED YOU, BOY. WE'VE NEVER MET!

PULL THE OTHER ONE, MEAN GREEN!

YOU TOLD US THAT THERE'S *NOTHING* YOU DON'T KNOW ABOUT THE FUTURE, OR THE PAST! I AND MY *THUNDERCATS* VISIT HERE IN A FEW YEARS TIME, WHEN YOU'RE DISGUISED AS THE GREAT PHARAOH *KA-REY-BAR!*

OH? AND DO WE MEET AT ANY *OTHER* TIME?

YOU AND I ARE IN *CONSTANT* BATTLE ON *THIRD* EART-*WAIT!* YOU DIDN'T KNOW *ANY* OF THIS...

... AND I'VE JUST TOLD YOU ALL YOU *NEEDED* TO KNOW!

INDEED, CUBLING–ALL I NEED TO KNOW TO *FINISH* YOU BEFORE YOU HAVE THE CHANCE TO THWART MY PLANS!

SHESSH!

NOT IF I CAN DODGE YOUR *ENERGY BLAST*, YOU VILLAIN! YOU DON'T GET A *SECOND* CHANCE...

YOU MAY INDEED BE *RIGHT*, VERMIN...

... BUT ON THE *OTHER* HAND...

ARRHH!

56

ELSEWHEN...

THE STINGERS ARE *SCAVENGERS*. THEY STEAL OUR *CHILDREN*, OUR *YOUNG CATTLE* ...THEY LIVE ON HIGH ROCKS, WEBBING THEIR NESTS...

WHERE *IS* THIS PLACE? I WALK INTO THE *CAVE OF THE VORTEX*, AND NEXT I'M IN SOME *VOLCANIC WASTE-LAND*...

THIS IS *VOLCANO LAKE* - AND THE CAVE OF THE VORTEX IS OVER TO THE *WEST*...

BUT THE CAVE OF THE VORTEX IS SURROUNDED BY *SNOW*, NOT LAVA! SOMEHOW I'VE BEEN WARPED INTO SOME *ALTERNATIVE* VERSION OF THIS STRANGE PLANET...

TELL ME- THIS *IS* THIRD EARTH, ISN'T IT?

INDEED *NOT*, CHEETARA. THIS IS *EARTH MINUS THREE!*

I *UNDERSTAND* NOW. I AM FROM THIS PLANET'S FAR *FUTURE*. I AM OF THE NOBLE *THUNDERCATS*, WHO COME HERE TO DO GREAT DEEDS...

...AND I WILL SAVE YOUR *CHILDREN!*

A LONG AND ARDUOUS CLIMB LIES AHEAD...

THIS WIND- CUTS LIKE A *KNIFE!* MUSTN'T GIVE UP...!

CAT LADY!

THERE THEY *ARE!*

UH-OH! I WAS HOPING TO GET THEM OUT *WITHOUT* MOTHER CREEPY-CRAWLY NOTICING. LOOKS LIKE I'VE BLOWN *THAT* ONE...

HISSNNN..?

Y-YOU'VE NOT BEATEN ME *YET*, MUMM-RA!

I DON'T *HAVE* TO, CUBLING...

...YOU SEE— YOU'RE *LEAVING!*

THE BATTLE OUTSIDE GOES *BADLY* FOR MY THUGRONS. PERHAPS IT IS TIME TO PUT SOME OF THE *INFORMATION* THE CUB GAVE ME TO GOOD USE...

...SUCH AS THAT LITTLE NUGGET ABOUT—

ANOTHER IDENTITY!

LET HOSTILITIES *CEASE!* EVIL MUMM-RA HAS *FALLEN!* THE HERO LION-O HAS INSTRUCTED *ME* TO HELP YOU THROUGH YOUR TROUBLED TIMES...

WHO ARE *YOU?*

I AM *PHARAOH KA-REY-BAR.* AND NOW...SHALL WE BEGIN BY FINISHING THIS *PYRAMID*—SO THAT I MAY HAVE SOMEWHERE TO RULE YOU *JUSTLY* FROM...?

58

EARTH MINUS THREE.

N-NO GOOD— IT'S TOO BIG... TOO *STRONG!* CAN'T EVEN BREAK *FREE!*

PLEASE, CAT LADY! IF *YOU* CAN'T SAVE US, WE'RE *LOST!*

I— CAN'T— I—

EEEUGHH!

—I—CAN!

WHAK!

THOK!

KDOK!

PAINN!

YOU'RE CATCHING ON, WINGDING!

KRAWAK!

REMEMBER *THIS* THE NEXT TIME YOU FEEL LIKE KIDNAPPING HELPLESS CHILDREN!

COME ON, WHILE SHE'S **DAZED!**

GOING **DOWN!**

WHEEEE!

THANK YOU! THANK YOU FOR SAVING OUR CHILDREN!

HOW CAN WE **EVER** MAKE IT UP TO YOU?

NO **NEED** TO. SAVING YOUR CHILDREN WAS THE **LEAST** I COULD DO...

...UNTIL SOMEONE AROUND HERE INVENTS **INSECTICIDE**, THAT IS!

LOOK! UP IN THE SKY!

IT'S LIKE THE BADGE ON YOUR **DRESS**, CAT LADY!

YES—AND IT MEANS THAT **I** CAN GO HOME, TOO!

L-LION-O? IS THAT *YOU?*

NONE *OTHER!* LONG TIME NO *SEE,* CHEETARA!

'LONG TIME' IS RIGHT! IT WAS THE *VORTEX...*

... IT WASS INDEED I, TRAVELLERSSS. I SSPIN THROUGH *TIME ITSSELF*—SSOMETIMES GUESSTS ARE *LOSST* IN MY TIMELESSS PASSAGESSS...

WELL, I LEARNED THAT YOU CAN'T CHANGE THE PAST—AND *MEDDLING* ONLY MAKES IT *WORSE!*

I GUESS YOU COULD SAY I GOT A *BUZZ* OUT OF IT, TOO!

NOT THAT IT WASN'T *TOUGH* THERE FOR A MOMENT! I THOLGHT I WAS *DONE FOR* WHEN MUMM-RA BLASTED ME!

MUMM-RA COULD NOT *DESTROY* YOU BEFORE YOU HAD BEEN BORN—HE COULD ONLY CASST YOU OUT OF THE *TIME LINE,* SENDING YOU BACK *HERE...*

THAT'S A RELIEF—*NOW!*

WON'T YOU *SSTAY* A WHILE? SSAMPLE *ANOTHER* SSLICE OF HISSTORY. THE *MILLENIUM*—THE *CENTURY*—THE *MOMENT*—THE *VORTEXX* ISS YOUR GUIDE!

SOME *OTHER* TIME, MAYBE!

THE END...FOR *NOW!*

61